I am your pet

Best friends'

Rabbit

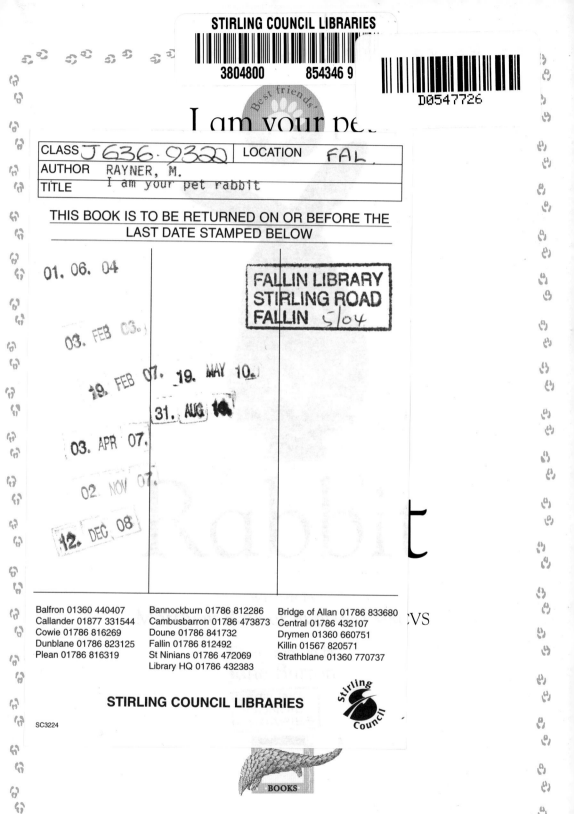

BOOKS

Editor: Annabel Blackledge
Art Editor: Kate Mullins
Editorial Director: Louise Pritchard
Design Director: Jill Plank

First published in Great Britain in 2004
by Pangolin Books
Unit 17, Piccadilly Mill, Lower Street,
Stroud, Gloucestershire, GL5 2HT

J 936·9322

A CIP catalogue record for this book is available
from the British Library.

ISBN 1-84493-006-8

Colour reproduction by Black Cat Graphics Ltd, Bristol, UK
Printed in England by Goodman Baylis Ltd

Ooooh,
I must look
my best!

Contents

My family

I come from a family of animals called lagomorphs. My closest relatives are wild rabbits and hares. I am just one of the many beautiful types of pet rabbit.

Are you ready to learn all about me?

Cotton tail
I have a short, fluffy tail. It is white underneath. Wild rabbits flash their tails to warn their friends of danger.

Fur coat
All rabbits have thick fur. My fur is short, but some pet rabbits have long fur.

A little help

You will need an adult to help you take care of me. He or she will make sure that we are both safe and well, and that we do not hurt each other by mistake. You can teach your adult helper everything you learn from this book.

Here I am

Back legs
I have very strong back legs. They help me to jump and run fast.

I am a good listener.

Ear we go
I have big, long ears. They are very good at picking up sounds. I can hear things that you cannot hear.

Full size
I was fully grown at about eight months old.

Built for speed
I am made to run fast and jump high. I need plenty of space to play in. If I am cooped up, I will feel sad and my long, strong legs will get stiff and weak.

Buck teeth
I have long front teeth to grasp food, and strong back teeth to grind it up. My teeth will go on growing all my life.

Twitchy nose
I have a good sense of smell. I use it to find out about other rabbits. All rabbits rub their chins on things to leave their scent. You cannot smell it, but we can.

Fluffy feet
I have five toes on my front paws and four on my back paws. I have claws on all my toes to help me dig and grip the ground when I run.

All shapes and sizes

Pet rabbits come in lots of shapes, sizes and colours.
Small ones weigh as little as 1 kg. Large ones can
weigh 10 kg. Some breeds of pet rabbit
are much better at running
and jumping than others.

Bunny breeds

Little characters
Different breeds of
rabbit have different
characters. The larger
breeds are usually
quieter than the
smaller breeds.

Hello my
floppy-eared
friend!

Dwarf Lop
This bunny friend
is a Dwarf Lop.
He has got floppy
ears. He is the most
popular type of
pet rabbit.

Angora
This is an Angora rabbit. She has a long, very fluffy coat. Even her ears are fluffy!

English Spot
My English Spot friend is named after his coat. It is white with spots. He is medium-size like me.

All kinds of ears

All rabbits have wonderful ears, but many of us have extra special ears. Some are floppy and some stand up straight. Some are furry, some are pointed, some are tiny and some are huge.

Netherland Dwarf
The Netherland Dwarf is one of the smallest rabbits, and has tiny, pointed ears.

All mixed up
I am a mixed-breed bunny. My parents were different breeds. I am just as beautiful as my pedigree friends.

Back to nature

Wild ways

Pet rabbits like me behave in
a similar way to our wild cousins.
We are lively and like to explore.
We prefer to eat first thing in the
morning and in the early evening,
which are the safest times in the wild.

LOOK OUT!

* **Do not** chase me
  when you want to
  pick me up. I may
  think you are hunting
  me. The more you
  chase me, the faster
  I will run.

Always alert
*We never stop
listening for sounds
of danger.*

Ready to run
*We can spring
into action in
a split second.
And we can
run fast to
escape from
danger.*

Dig deep
*We don't need
to dig burrows to
live in, but we still
love to dig holes
when you let us out
to play in the garden.*

Shhhh,
I think I can hear
someone coming.

Thumper
If I am scared,
I may thump a back
foot on the ground.
Wild rabbits do this to
warn their friends
of danger nearby.
This could be a
fox hunting for
his dinner.

Wild relations

Rabbits like to be with other rabbits.
In the wild, they live together in
burrows underground. During the
day they come out to eat and play.
They like to groom each other too.

Somewhere to live

Before you bring me home, you must get a hutch for me to live in. It must be large enough so that I can hop around in it. Make sure it will keep out the wind and rain. I will also need lots of dust-free bedding and a large outside run.

Getting ready

House rabbit

You can keep me in your house if you prefer. I will need a special indoor hutch to live in, but you can let me out to play when you are there to watch me.

Litter bun
You can train me to go to the toilet in a litter tray. Buy one that is large enough for me to sit in and some special rabbit litter. Put the tray where I usually go to the toilet.

Bedding down
Put a layer of wood shavings on the floor of my hutch and give me a pile of straw or hay to sleep in.

It's such thirsty work being a superstar!

Bunny bottle
You can get a special bottle for my water. It will clip to my hutch and will not spill like a bowl of water can.

Grooming kit
Buy a special rabbit brush for grooming me. Long-haired rabbits need to be groomed every day.

Food for thought
I will need a bowl that won't break if I throw it around. I will also need food, hay and some fresh vegetables to nibble.

Which rabbit?

Places to go

Buy your rabbit from an animal shelter or a rabbit breeder. Look out for adverts for rabbits needing good homes in pet shops and at vets' surgeries. Or look in your local newspaper.

Full of life
I am alert and lively. Choose a rabbit like me, not one that is very sleepy or quiet.

Fine fur
I keep my fur clean, so it is always soft and shiny. Your rabbit should have fur like mine.

Of course I've washed behind my ears!

I think we'd be perfect together!

Doe

Buck

Boys and girls

Decide whether you want a boy or a girl rabbit. Boys are called bucks and girls are called does. Bucks have two round openings under their tails. Does have a round opening and a small narrow one.

Friendly
Choose a friendly rabbit like me. I am playful and I love being petted.

All grown up
I am grown up and already tame and house-trained. I am much less work than a baby bunny.

Check up
Take me to the vet for a health check as soon as you get me. The vet will tell you whether I need any injections and will give you advice about caring for me.

Feed me!

Hooray for hay

The most important part of my diet is good-quality grass hay. Make sure I always have plenty of fresh hay and I will nibble on it happily all day.

Twice as nice!

It is good for me to eat my droppings. I do this to get as much goodness out of my food as possible.

> Oh goody, my favourite treat ... an apple.

LOOK OUT!

* **Never feed me** chocolate, sweet food or lawn clippings. They will upset my tummy.
* **Don't let me** get too fat. I won't be able to clean myself properly and might get infections.

Fresh and fruity

I need to eat fresh grass every day, if possible. It is good for my tummy and my teeth, and it keeps me busy. You can give me a bit of fresh fruit or vegetable each day, too.

Less is more

Feed me only small amounts of fruit. Half an apple a day is plenty. Any more could upset my tummy.

*Fruit and
vegetables*

Mixed food

Pellets

Something extra
*You can include a
bit of mixed rabbit
food or pellets in
my diet. Check the
packet to find out
how much to
give me.*

Delicate tummy
*If you want to change my
diet, do it gradually. A sudden
change will make me ill.*

Drink up
I need to have fresh water
to drink all the time. It helps
me to digest my food properly.
Please change my drinking
water every day.

Naturally clean
I am naturally a clean animal. I will go to the toilet in mainly one area of my hutch. If you train me to use a litter tray, it will be easy to keep my hutch clean.

Scoop

Wood shavings

Hay

A tidy home

Why and when

You must clean out my hutch at least once a week. Dirty bedding can give me sore feet and breathing problems. It also attracts flies in the summer. The flies will lay eggs on me, which will make me very ill.

All the right stuff
You will need a scoop or a dustpan and brush to clean out my hutch. When it is clean, I will need a fresh supply of bedding and food.

Mmmm, I don't know whether to sleep in it or eat it!

LOOK OUT!
* **Don't use** scented or treated wood shavings. They may irritate my eyes and lungs and make my feet sore.
* **Never use** bleach or other chemical cleaners in my hutch. It will burn my skin and paws.

The know how

Put me in my run in the garden or in another safe place while you clean out my hutch. Remove all my old bedding and food. Clean the hutch with weak disinfectant, then let it dry.

Scoop it up
Use a scoop to take droppings and any wet bedding out of my hutch every day.

Freshen up
If you give me hay to sleep in, I will probably eat most of it. Give me a large handful of fresh hay each day.

I am all ears!

Reading the signs

Rabbits talk to each other using their bodies. I will talk to you this way too. As you get to know me you will learn my body language. Then you will know when I am happy, angry or scared, just from the way I behave.

Nasty noises
If I am angry or scared, I may growl or hiss. I might even charge at you and try to bite you. If I am badly injured you might hear me scream.

Who's there?
If I stand up tall with my ears pricked, it means that I am feeling alert and curious.

LOOK OUT!
* **If I am** very quiet and grind my teeth, I may be ill or in pain. Take me to the vet.
* **If I become** naughty or fierce, I may be bored. Play with me more and give me things to do in my hutch.

Bunny bliss

When I am happy I often purr like a cat. You may hear me purr when you stroke and groom me. If I am pleased to see you or want to play I will chase you or jump around.

Chilling out
When a rabbit is tired or just very relaxed, he will flop down on the floor and spread himself out.

Rabbit habits

Clean noses are best for twitching.

Wash time
I groom myself and my bunny friends only when I feel relaxed and safe. If you are lucky, I might try to groom you too!

Making friends

I may be timid when you first get me. You must give me time to get to know you. When I feel I can trust you I will let you handle me. Don't try to pick me up until I am ready. Wait for me to come to you.

A friend for life

Oooh, don't stop. That feels lovely.

The gentle touch
Stroke me gently on my head. This lets me know that you only want to be my friend and will not hurt me.

LOOK OUT!
* **Never try** to grab me. You will startle me.
* **Never pick** me up by my ears. This will hurt me.
* **Never hit** me if I have been naughty. I will not know what I have done wrong and you will just frighten me.

Pick me up

You must pick me up properly so that you do not hurt my back. Put one hand under my bottom. Hold on to my chest with your other hand so that you don't drop me.

Carry me
Hold me close to your body when you carry me, but not too tightly. If I struggle a lot, try wrapping me in a towel. I will feel safe, and will not be able to scratch you.

Rabbit treats and chews

Training treats

When you are training me or making friends, give me a tasty treat to help me understand. You can use pieces of fresh vegetable or fruit or treats from a pet shop.

Busy bunny

I am very inquisitive and get bored easily if I don't have anything to eat or investigate. Give me some toys to play with and things to nibble. Let me explore new places too.

Home and

Okay Mr Snail, let's have a race!

Come inside

As well as playing outside, I will enjoy coming inside your home. I will sniff around, have a good run and might even lie down next to you while you are watching television.

Part of the family

I will want to be where you are. Let me follow you around while you tidy your room or hang out the washing. I will soon feel like part of the family.

LOOK OUT!

* **Never let** me run around indoors all alone. I might ruin the furniture and carpets, or hurt myself.
* **Never leave** me on my own outdoors. I might dig or chew my way out of my run or under the fence.

garden

The great outdoors

My wild cousins spend most of their time outside in the fresh air. I need to spend time outside too. There's nothing I like better than nibbling a few dandelions, running round the lawn then flopping down for a nap.

Tunnels and pots
Put tunnels and pots in my run. I will dash through them and climb on them.

No one has to tell me to eat up my greens.

Playing safe
Keep me safe from cats, dogs and foxes when I am out playing.

Fun with food
Wild rabbits spend hours every day munching on plants and grasses, and I am happy to do the same. You can even hide bits of food around my hutch. I love hunting and scrabbling for tasty titbits.

Daily check-ups

I will probably stay very healthy if you care for me properly. But there are some common illnesses and problems I can have. I may become very ill if you let them get worse, so give me a check-up every day. Take me to the vet regularly for vaccinations.

Health matters

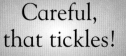

Careful, that tickles!

Coat and skin
When you groom me, check that I don't have bald patches or flaky skin. If I am scratching a lot, I may have fleas or mites.

Ear checks
Look in my ears for sore spots and wax. Never put anything in my ears unless the vet tells you to.

Getting to know me
It is very important that you get to know me well and learn all my usual habits. Then you will notice if I am feeling ill, because I will behave differently.

Mmmm, much tastier than toothpaste!

Bright eyes
Check that my eyes are clean and bright. Sometimes my tears don't drain away properly, and this can cause problems with my eyes.

Teeth checks
Give me fruit-tree twigs to chew to help keep my teeth healthy. If I am dribbling or cannot eat properly, my teeth may be hurting me.

LOOK OUT!
* **Look out** for fly eggs and maggots on me. They can kill me. If you see any, take me to the vet quickly.
* **Go straight** to the vet if I sneeze a lot or have a runny nose. I could have snuffles.

Bottom check
Check my bottom twice a day. Clean it if it is dirty. Take me to the vet to find out why it is getting dirty.

I need a friend

I need company most of the time or I will get lonely and bored. I like making friends with dogs, guinea pigs and other rabbits, but never introduce me to a cat. It might try to eat me!

Two's

My mate
I like guinea pigs. We can play together if you keep an eye on us, but we should eat and sleep separately.

Gently does it
I usually get on well with dogs, but always keep a close eye on us.

Fast learner
A puppy will learn quickly how to behave around me. She might even let me be the boss!

Company

Oh baby!
Do not keep a buck and a doe together – they will have lots of babies!

Will you share your daisy with me?

You and me
If I live by myself, I will need you to be my best friend. You should come and say hello to me as often as you can and play with me every day.

Best friends

Two rabbits living together usually become best friends.
They will hop around after each other and lie down
together. They will groom each other too. If your rabbits
fight, ask your vet for some advice.

Mummy bunny

A female rabbit, or doe, can start breeding at four months old. A male rabbit, or buck, can start breeding at five months old. The babies are called kittens. A doe can have more than 50 kittens a year!

Baby bunnies

Don't touch!
Never handle young kittens or disturb their nest. The mother may get scared and reject them. Give her plenty to eat and lots of peace and quiet.

New baby
Kittens are born blind, deaf and hairless. They drink milk from their mother. At one week, kittens have some fur, but they still cannot see or hear.

Starting out
Three-week-old kittens can see and hear. They begin to eat food, but need their mother's milk until they are six weeks old.

LOOK OUT!
* **Rabbits can** have lots of babies very quickly. It is best for your rabbit if your vet gives her an operation so she cannot have babies.

I can't wait for them to leave home!

Happy families
When the kittens start to leave the nest to explore, you can begin to handle them. Young rabbits are very playful and like to investigate. They can get into trouble, so keep an eye on them.

Ready for re-homing
Rabbits can be separated from their mother when they are six weeks old. They are ready to go to a new home at nine weeks. At this stage, they look like small versions of their parents, but they still have a lot of growing to do.

Glossary

bedding
The material a rabbit sleeps on is his bedding. Wood shavings topped with straw or hay make the best bedding.

breed
A breed is a type of rabbit. There are lots of different breeds of rabbit – Angora and Dwarf Lop are just two of them.

buck
A male rabbit is called a buck.

burrow
Wild rabbits live in holes in the ground called burrows.

doe
A female rabbit is called a doe.

fly strike
When flies lay eggs on a rabbit and they hatch into maggots it is known as fly strike. This is very dangerous for rabbits.

grooming
When an animal's fur is gently brushed to remove any dust or dirt, it is called grooming.

handling
Handling is when you pick up or touch a rabbit. There is a special way to handle rabbits so that you do not hurt them.

hay
Hay is dried grass. It is full of goodness and keeps longer than fresh grass.

hutch
Pet rabbits live in special cages called hutches.

kitten
A baby rabbit is called a kitten.

lagomorph
Rabbits belong to the family of animals called lagomorphs.

pregnant
When a female rabbit is pregnant it means that she has got babies growing inside her.

veterinary surgeon
A veterinary surgeon, or vet, is an animal doctor. You should take a rabbit to see a vet if it is ill or injured.

Find out more

Websites

www.pdsa.org.uk
Information on responsible pet care and how to join the PDSA's Pet Protectors club.

www.houserabbit.co.uk
Official website for the Rabbit Welfare Association, with an online shop and a cute rabbit photo gallery.

www.rspca.org.uk
Go to the animal care page on rabbits for advice on caring for a rabbit.

What a lot of information!

Addresses

PDSA
Whitechapel Way
Priorslee
Telford
Shropshire, TF2 9PQ

Rabbit Welfare Association
PO Box 603
Horsham
West Sussex, RH13 5WL

RSPCA
Wilberforce Way
Southwater
Horsham
West Sussex, RH13 9RS

Index

Picture credits
t=top b=bottom m=middle l=left r=right

Warren Photographic: 7tr, 7tm, 7mr, 8br, 9t, 10tr, 17br, 19tr, 27tm, 27b, 28ml, 28br, 29t, 29br